Mosquitoes and Wrigglers

by Vita Jimenez

![Harcourt]

Orlando   Boston   Dallas   Chicago   San Diego

Visit *The Learning Site!*

www.harcourtschool.com

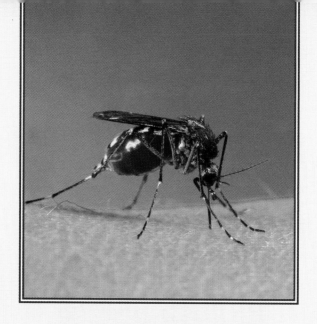

What Is a Mosquito?

Summer is here! The weather is getting hot. It's time for some outdoor fun. A game of catch sounds great. Just as you raise your hand to catch that ball, you stop.

Scratch! Scratch! Scratch! You look down. There is a little red spot on your arm. It itches so much. You're already grumbling. You have a mosquito bite.

If someone said you didn't have a mosquito bite, you'd say that was nonsense. It's true, though. Why? Because mosquitoes don't really bite! What *does* happen?

A mosquito sticks you with its mouth. Its mouth is sharp like a needle. It is hollow like a straw. Through its mouth, the mosquito can sip a tiny bit of your blood.

Why do mosquitoes sip blood? How does a mosquito find you at night? Are mosquitoes just up to mischief? Can a mosquito really do harm to a person? Or is a mosquito just an annoying little pest?

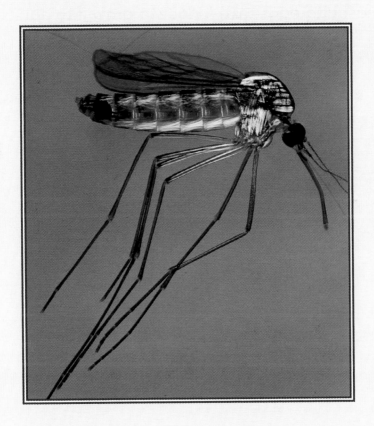

Mosquitoes belong to the group of insects called flies. Flies that have one pair of wings are called *true flies*. The mosquito and the housefly are true flies. Dragonflies and mayflies have two pairs of wings. They're not true flies.

True flies are found all over the world. They live in warm climates and cold climates. In warm climates, mosquito eggs change into adult mosquitoes in a week. In colder climates, mosquito eggs take longer to grow into adults.

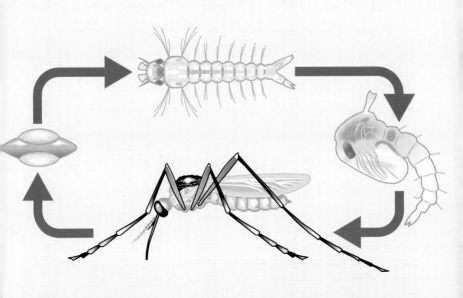

🌀 The Life Cycle of a Mosquito

The life of a mosquito has four stages. First, the mosquito is an egg. Second, it is a larva. Third, it is a pupa. Fourth, it is an adult. Mosquitoes look very different at each stage.

Only female mosquitoes "bite," or sip blood. Some sip blood from animals such as cows or horses. Some sip blood from frogs or snakes. Others sip blood from people.

Male mosquitoes are harmless. They do not need blood. Male mosquitoes sip the juice from plants and flowers.

5

Female mosquitoes lay their eggs in a swamp or a pond. They need to lay their eggs in water that is still, or not moving.

Sometimes rain water collects in empty watering cans. It may collect in the dishes under flowerpots. It may collect in old tires or in barrels. A female mosquito can lay her eggs in any still water.

Mosquito Eggs

The larva is the second stage in the life cycle. The larva of a mosquito is called a *wriggler*. A wriggler moves by jerking its body back and forth. A wriggler looks like a tiny worm.

Wrigglers eat tiny things that live in the water. Sometimes wrigglers eat other wrigglers!

A wriggler can open its jaws to eat. It can chew its food. This is something that adult mosquitoes cannot do.

A wriggler needs air. It has a little air tube at the end of its body. A wriggler sticks the tube up above the water to get air. The rest of the wriggler stays under the water.

Mosquito Pupa

Wrigglers grow quickly. They may shed their skins four times in four to ten days. After a wriggler sheds for the last time, it becomes a pupa.

A mosquito pupa is shaped a little like a comma. The head and part of the body are rolled into a tiny ball. The bottom part of the body is curved. A thin skin covers the body.

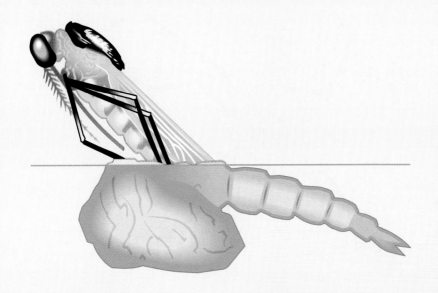

A mosquito pupa does not eat. It changes into an adult in three to four days. When the adult is ready to come out, the skin of the pupa splits down the back. The adult pushes its head and front legs out. Then the rest of its body comes out.

When the mosquito comes out, its wings are still wet. When its wings are dry, the mosquito will be able to fly. Most mosquitoes do not fly more than a mile away.

A male mosquito lives about ten days. Female mosquitoes can live as long as forty days.

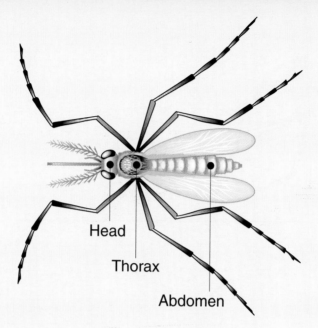

Head

Thorax

Abdomen

🖼 The Body of a Mosquito

A mosquito has three parts to its body. One part is the head. One part is the thorax. One part is the abdomen. The head has eyes, mouth parts, and two antennae. The thorax has legs and wings. The abdomen is attached to the thorax.

A mosquito has a round head and two large eyes. Its eyes cover most of its head. Mosquitoes' eyes are made up of thousands of lenses. Each lens has six sides. The eyes let a mosquito see things move. It cannot see things clearly, though.

A mosquito has two antennae, or feelers. These antennae are between the eyes. Antennae help mosquitoes hear and smell. Mosquitoes can even pick up the smell of your breath and your body with their antennae. That's how they find an animal — day or night.

Female mosquitoes have antennae that are covered with soft, fine hair. Male mosquitoes have antennae that are covered with thicker hair.

Antennae

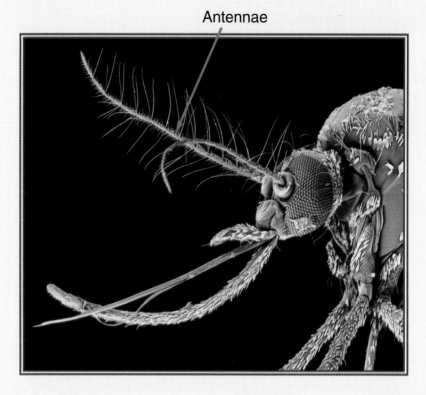

A mosquito has a mouth like a tube. The tube is called a *proboscis*. In the proboscis are sharp needle parts. These needle parts can puncture, or break through, the skin. They let the mosquito sip blood. Mosquitoes can only drink. All of their food is liquid. That is because adult mosquitoes have no jaws.

Like all insects, a mosquito has six legs. Each leg has a claw with a hairy, sticky pad. The claws and pads are what help a mosquito cling to ceilings. Mosquitoes can even walk upside down.

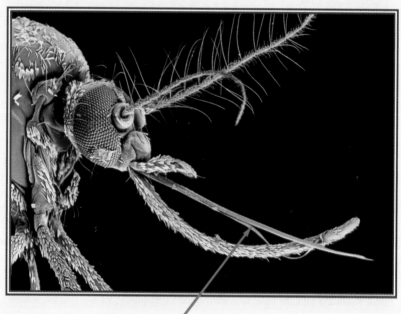

Proboscis

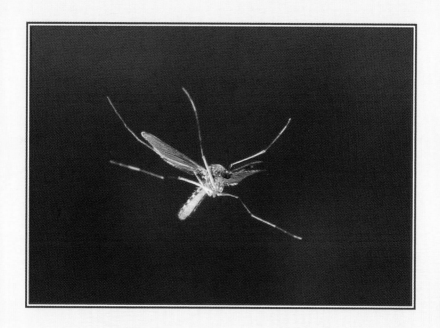

A mosquito has one pair of wings. A mosquito beats its wings when it lifts itself into the air. It has to keep beating them to stay in the air. The wings of a mosquito move 1,000 times a minute!

Instead of a second pair of wings, a mosquito has two little rods with knobs at each end. These rods wiggle when the mosquito flies. When a mosquito is close to you, you hear a noise like a buzz or a whine. This noise is made by the mosquito's moving wings and wiggling rods.

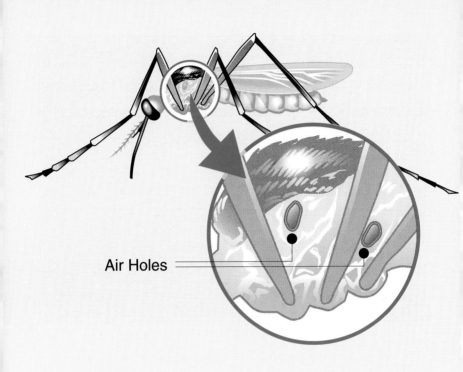

Air Holes

A mosquito needs to breathe. It does this through small holes along the sides of its body. A mosquito has a total of twenty holes that carry air to all parts of its body. Two pairs of holes are on the thorax, and eight pairs are along the abdomen. Some kinds of mosquitoes have a pointy abdomen. Others have a rounded abdomen.

Even with three body parts, most mosquitoes are less than 1/4 inch long.

Too Many Mosquitoes

Dragonflies are the natural enemies of mosquitoes. They eat mosquitoes. Other natural enemies are spiders, frogs, fish, bats, lizards, and birds. They all enjoy mosquito tidbits! Nature helps control how many mosquitoes there are in one place.

Sometimes mosquitoes carry germs that cause diseases. Mosquitoes may be a problem for some towns. If a place has too many mosquitoes, something needs to be done.

WARNING
MOSQUITO
HAZARD
Remove all
standing water

People on a town council may meet to decide what to do about a mosquito problem. The council may ask everyone to get rid of standing water where mosquitoes might lay eggs. Then it is everyone's duty to follow the rules of the council. A summons and a fine may be given to anyone who does not follow the rules.

People need to work together to solve the problem of too many mosquitoes. Maybe, when you grow up, you will be a scientist. Maybe you can figure out what to do about too many mosquitoes.